DEEMS TAYLOR

STUDIES

OF

CONTEMPORARY
AMERICAN COMPOSERS

BY

JOHN TASKER HOWARD

DEEMS TAYLOR

.25

1927

J. FISCHER & BRO., NEW YORK

119 WEST 40TH STREET

PRINTED IN U.S.A.

The author desires to express his gratitude
to his friend and colleague, Paul Kempf, for
his collaboration in preparing the biographical
data contained in these pages.

J. T. H.

DEEMS TAYLOR

DEEMS TAYLOR

I

THERE is probably no man in America who has done more of benefit to the profession of composing in this country than has Deems Taylor, for through his own personal success he has both proved and disproved certain definite impressions which have clung traditionally to the composers' craft, thereby clearing a path that will make it far easier for others to proceed to worth-while achievement in what has to date been classed as the least favored of all arts.

He has proved that well-directed musical talent, plus those qualities generally prescribed by exploiters of success-methods, will find its way to fame even in these allegedly cold-tempered United States.

He has proved that here a composer may raise himself by the boot-straps and, suffering an avoidance of cheap sensationalism, establish himself a figure in the general news of the day.

He has proved that a man may be essentially practical in his manner of living, thinking and working and yet achieve international distinction as a creator of highly imaginative music.

He has proved that versatility is no bar to special success—has smashed the old saw that if you are a jack of all trades you must, forsooth, be a master of none.

He has proved that there is a substantial market in this land of industry, commerce and finance for products of purely artistic calibre; that there is a living to be made out of composition.

Apply reverse English to these things he has proved by his own record of accomplishment, and obviously your answer is what he has disproved. Now, add the consideration that he has destroyed the image so popularly prevalent that good composers must be æsthetic, pale-skinned, long-haired and rather effeminate individuals, alternately rhapsodic and morose, constantly publishing their complaint against a public that neither understands nor appreciates them, and the case assumes completion.

II

Deems Taylor is a mild-mannered person, of medium height, inclined toward baldness, wears glasses, has what novelists describe as well-chiselled features illumined by an expression of intentness, emphasized by a firmly set lower jaw. As a man he sizes up extremely well in a group of five, reading from left to right, showing the Americans who had this past Spring been awarded Doctor's degrees by a great American University. His companions in this distinguished cluster were the Chairman of the General Electric Company's Board, the President of the American Museum of Natural History, the Secretary of State in President Coolidge's cabinet, and the professor of literature at Yale University.

In the eyes of his intimates the address of seriousness which he presents to casual observers is but a mask. For they know him best as a man of unfailing good humor, a philosopher who delights in the whimsicalities of life and knows both how to fashion and enjoy a joke.

Mention has been made of Deems Taylor's versatility. It is not merely that he can do many things but it is because he does them all superlatively well that this characteristic deserves stressing. At various times he has functioned with outstanding success as a newspaper-man, as critic, as linguist, as translator of prose and poetry, as an artist capable of handling the brush and pen with signal facility, as editor, as public speaker; and as a composer.

In the field of journalism, both in his technical musical criticisms and in his articles on practical musical subjects he writes with clarity of style, with matured authority and with disarming frankness and sincerity. Here again his engaging spirit of good humor finds expression to lighten the burden of his message.

III

It is interesting to trace the steps by which Taylor advanced himself to a position described by Dr. George Alexander, president of the Council of New York University, as "one of the foremost of the living composers."

Deems Taylor is one of those rarest of residents of New York who was actually born in that city. His arrival was dated just three days before Christmas in the year 1885. He made his elementary studies at the Ethical Culture School and graduated to New York University, where his many-sided talents brought him a conspicuous participation in under-graduate activities. The records do not show it, but one takes it for granted that he penned the sketches which adorned the year book of his class. Probably he also wrote the sonnet which a distracted editor called for to fill half a page needed to complete a folio. At fraternity smokers he could always be relied upon to entertain; his inimitable burlesque on grand opera, using as his "props" a varied assortment of straw and felt hats, was certain to put the crowd in good humor.

The record does show, however, that in association with a class-mate, William LeBaron, who in later years was responsible for the libretto of *Apple Blossoms*, the farce, *The Very Idea*, and numerous other plays, Taylor wrote the music for four comic operas during his collegiate term. One of them, *The Echo*, was considered good enough by Charles Dillingham, the theatrical producer, to merit a Broadway presentation, in which Bessie McCoy was starred.

The innate desire for an adequate means of musical expression must have reached its peak in the young man's consciousness some five years after his graduation from college, for it was at that period that he undertook the serious study of harmony and counterpoint. In the meantime he was struggling with the more serious problems of life, trying to reconcile the meagre salary paid to budding journalists with the ever-rising cost of living.

One knows that this storm and stress period did exist in his life; his own confessions, however, furnish but inadequate data upon which to draw comparisons with similar experiences in the biographies of other celebrated composers. His journalistic lineage carries him through the editorship of a house organ, a brief engagement as conductor of a humorous column in the now defunct "New York Press," the inevitable period of unemployment (attendant to all newspaper careers); assistant editorship of the "New York Tribune's" Sunday magazine; correspondent in France for the "Tribune," in 1916 and 1917; associate editor of "Collier's Weekly" from 1917 until 1919; and music critic of the New York "World" from 1921 to 1925. In August, 1927, he became editor of "Musical America."

Whether from natural inclination or from pressure of circumstances, the early studies he had made in harmony and counterpoint under Oscar Coon were not logically followed by directed guidance in composition, instrumentation, and other subjects, designed to prepare one for the career of composer. His sole researches along these lines were self-made. As a composer he is self-instructed, and it is the opinion of reliable critics that he made an extremely good job of it. His studies in musical history were sufficiently profound to equip him to give a series of lectures on this subject in 1919 in Denver, Colo.

It was at this time that he formed a close friendship with Percy Rector Stephens, the New York vocal instructor and then conductor of the Schumann Club. Stephens had confidence in the Taylor talent and lost no opportunity to promote the young man's progress. The purpose of the Schumann Club, it will be recalled, was to deliver programs for women's vocal ensemble that would follow as closely as possible the canons dictating the structure of artist recital programs. To achieve this laudable enterprise it was necessary to adapt the music and render translated texts of an entire library for the club. Mr. Taylor undertook the task with enthusiasm and the product of his labors was among his first essays in musical-literary effort to court serious critical attention.

The prize contest for composers, of which we have so many now-a-days and which are so frequently condemned for their failures to produce a National school of outstanding creative genius, seems, nevertheless to find its associations in the biographies of the current class of American composers. It was through this means, by winning the first place in the National Federation of Music Clubs competition in 1913, with his orchestral composition *The Siren Song*, that Taylor attracted his first recognition as a serious writer in the larger forms. Within three years he had added to his output, in addition to numerous songs with piano accompaniment, *Two Studies in Rhythm* for piano (Op. 5, Nos. 1 and 2); *The Chambered Nautilus* (Op. 7), a cantata for mixed chorus and orchestra based on the poem of Oliver Wendell Holmes; *The Highwayman* (Op. 8), a cantata for women's voices and orchestra, to the poem of Alfred Noyes; and a song cycle, *The City of Joy*, to the poem by Charles Hanson Towne. In *The Highwayman*, written especially for the MacDowell Festival in Peterboro, N. H., in 1914, Taylor gave his first evidence of that trait that was subsequently accepted as one of his native characteristics, namely his ability to sense public taste. No student of his record can escape consideration of this conspicuous talent in his craft. *The Highwayman* soon found its place among the most popular works in this form in our current music literature and the name and fame of Deems Taylor grew accordingly. He had raised himself immeasurably from the file of dilettante composers, and discriminating critics began to look to him for works of lasting importance.

In this respect they were not to be disappointed. Early in 1917 there came from his pen an orchestral work, which, through sheer interest and merit forced itself into the repertoires of all of our leading symphony organizations: *Through the Looking Glass*. The first performance in New York proved an event of signal interest in the news of the day and critics agreed that Taylor had fully lived up to the promise which his earlier efforts had offered. Within a few months orchestras in Paris and London had adopted the work, and thus he won his first recognition among the few American writers who have had performances abroad. The personal letters which Taylor received from several of the greatest contemporary musicians both here and abroad, on the strength of this music, may not be published; they show, however, that he was now accepted by them as one of them. His standing was secure.

Interrupting the output of works in the larger forms the record shows numerous songs, many of which were taken up with avidity by our leading concert singers and which will be discussed later from a different angle.

The Portrait of a Lady, a rhapsody for strings, wind and the piano, was the next of his more ambitious essays to win popular approval.

IV

As a practical man Taylor realized that if he were to continue his growth in serious music, he must find the means of livelihood in avenues which offered a more immediate return in the currency of the realm. He turned to the theatre and probably not without a feeling that here he would find also the fundamentals upon which he might some day build a work in the music drama form. It was an inviting undertaking, offering both income and working materials for future development. In 1922 he wrote the incidental music for Austin Strong's pantomime *A Man About Town*, which graduated from the Comedy Club to the Ritz Theatre. He had "broken into" the theatrical game and now according to the custom of the Rialto, he was to be pursued instead of being himself the pursuer in the quest for commissions.

Liliom required music; Deems Taylor was the logical man to supply it. A score was needed for the farce-comedy, *Dulcy;* who better than Taylor could do it? In quick succession he added to the list incidental music for the Winthrop Ames production, *Will Shakespeare*, music for the Theatre Guild's *The Adding Machine*, a musical setting for Alan Seager's *I Have a Rendezvous with Death,* in George Tyler's production of *Humoresque;* the incidental music for *Rita Coventry;* incidental music for Gilbert Miller's production of *Cazanova;* incidental music for *Beggar on Horseback,* produced by Winthrop Ames in January, 1924, in which was introduced the pantomime *A Kiss in Xanadu;* and the score for the motion picture *Janice Meredith.*

The distinguished use to which Taylor later put the technic he had acquired in these excursions into the theatre, saves them from classification as "pot-boilers." And, what is more to the point, the music itself which he had written for these various productions, was of a quality which calls for no apologetic comment. Again he had shown his versatility and again he had added to the stature of his name as a creative artist.

During the period of prolific productivity in the theatre Taylor's addresses to the audiences of the formal concert halls were less frequent. Three outstanding works, however, found expression amid the whirl of activity attendant upon daily reviews of musical performances for his paper "The World," with his work often interrupted by conferences with producers, scenario writers, playwrights, actors, managers and others, to say nothing of the supervision of rehearsals. These contributions were the song for baritone, *Captain Stratton's Fancy,* a setting of the John Masefield poem; the symphonic poem, *Jurgen* (Op. 17); and the suite for Jazz Orchestra, *Circus Day* (Op. 18), for which the resourceful Ferdie Grofè was called upon to supply the orchestral arrangement.

Jurgen offers additional support to the contention made in the opening paragraphs of this record. It is another example of the service rendered by Deems Taylor to the cause of the American composer, for it represents one of the pioneer instances in which a conductor of an American symphony orchestra has sought out an American composer and commissioned him to write music for specific performance. Our composers had accustomed themselves to regard our symphony orchestras and their conductors as stumbling blocks in the road of progress. Taylor, in company with George Gershwin and Henry K. Hadley, and with the far-seeing Walter Damrosch as the instigator, was help-ing, then and there, to change a securely established custom. The orchestra was to go after the composer; and this shatter-ing of precedent is of far greater consequence than may seem apparent to casual observance of the facts.

For the same reason the attitude of the Metropolitan Opera Company toward the American composer and toward home-made opera, is a subject which offers unlimited opportunities for conjecture. Proof of an open-minded policy, a sincere desire to bring forth the best that was to be had, is afforded by the action (during the Winter of 1925) of the Board of Directors in com-missioning Deems Taylor, on the strength of his achievements in other musical forms, to compose an opera which would be prom-ised a production. No restrictions were placed upon him: The choice of a libretto was left entirely in his hands.

Note again the part which Deems Taylor was playing in the breaking down of traditional methods to set the function of the native composer in a new light.

When this call came to him, he determined to sacrifice every other of his manifold activities to a successful prosecution of the mission. Reluctantly he gave up the duties of music critic—a position in which he was fast winning sympathetic and wide-spread approval, even as the successor of the late James Gibbons Huneker.

He turned with enthusiasm and high hopes to the task of finding a libretto, a search which promised no easy fulfillment, for little had been done in this land to stimulate the production of operatic books that would satisfy the complex requirements of the lyric stage.

Acting upon his own frequently expressed conviction that a genuinely poetic and dramatic libretto is an indispensable adjunct to the score of a grand opera, Mr. Taylor turned for assistance to Edna St. Vincent Millay, whose volumes *Renascence*, *Second April*, *A Few Figs From Thistles*, and *The Harp Weaver* have established her as one of the few great lyric poets of this generation. Miss Millay's response to the appeal was an idea based upon a mediaeval legend; it was the story of *The King's Henchman*, and it made a strong appeal to Taylor's inherent sense of public taste. He could discover in it those elements which meant operatic success. He bade Miss Millay to go on with its development and meantime he busied himself with the laying out of his patterns.

Two years later, on the evening of February 17th, 1927, the world première of *The King's Henchman* took place at the Metro-politan Opera House. This was no ordinary première, even as brilliant as such events usually are. For months in advance the sagacious press department of the big theatre, aided enthusiasti-cally by a sympathetic press, had aroused public interest in the production. The "Evening Post" declared that "Never in the history of the Metropolitan Opera House had a native offering been attended by such advance interest and such good omens of success as *The King's Henchman*."

At the opera house, in the corridors, on the stage, back in the executive offices, everywhere there existed a spirit of expect-ancy and optimistic hope.

Tickets for the opening night were at a premium; on the final day they were unpurchasable at any price. Again Deems Taylor was making news.

The evening itself measured up fully to the anticipation it had created. It went into the records as one of the most dazzling of operatic premières; the audience actually liked the perform-ance as an opera; it seemed to enjoy itself hugely and there was accordingly wild enthusiasm when the composer and librettist were called to the front.

What was the effect of all this adulation, this frenzied praise upon the man who was responsible for the success of the evening? Again we turn to his intimates for the answer. We find him reading, deeply solicitous, those words of criticism which mea-sured with scientific analysis, in a more discriminating vein, the points of weakness in the score. He was neither professionally "high hat" nor "up-stage." It was his first grand opera and he knew that he had yet to learn. He felt that he could learn most from those who were prepared to show him how to step higher. He absorbed these comments with none of the petulance of the prima donna who finds in unfavorable criticism only the traces of jealousy and lack of appreciation.

V

But most convincing of all in the testimony relating to the outcome of the eventful evening's proceedings, was the decision of the Metropolitan Board of Directors, announced a few days after the première, to commission Taylor to write a second opera to be produced within two years from the date of his operatic debut.

Some idea of the public interest aroused through this promise of a second opera from Deems Taylor's pen was reflected in the large amount of space devoted to the project by the daily papers. For several months after the announcement there was interested speculation both in musical circles and in the newspapers over the choice of his libretto. It was not until late in the Fall that Mr. Taylor, in a column interview, gave out the news that had been awaited with such lively anticipation; his manner of acquainting the world with his selection was thoroughly characteristic.

The opera was to be based on an American novel, the identity of which at that time, remained a mystery. But Mr. Taylor's practical collaborator—his librettist—was to be none other than himself!

"I have found," the composer related to a reporter for the Associated Press, "the most charming and compatible, the most accomplished and erudite of collaborators. We get along splendidly together. It is true that I fuss and say crude things to this collaborator, sometimes, but it is all taken in good grace."

This same interview revealed another phase of the Taylor character, too significant to be overlooked in any discussion that pretends to reveal the man.

He declared that his new opera would be a product of the great city; that he had no tolerance for the widely exploited quiet of the country generally believed to be indispensable to those engaged in creative endeavor.

"I tried the country," he confided to his interviewer, "and it is too noisy. There are katydids, tree-toads, crickets, week-end guests and mosquitoes; all terrible noise-makers. Besides, New York is the only place I can be alone. In New York visitors stay ten minutes. In the country they stay ten days."

As to the nature of the new opera the composer described it as tragic-comic; half phantasy and half realism. "It has over-tones of romance and nuances of practical life," he said. "The emotions are typically American."

When the new owners of the weekly periodical, "Musical America," in search of an outstanding figure in the field of musical literature, one who would merit a sympathetic response from the musical public, selected Taylor for the post of editor-in-chief, they did no more than to reflect the high esteem that he had won for himself. The manner in which he took over the responsibility, as revealed in his declaration of intentions, in the issue of August 27th, 1927, was thoroughly characteristic of the man. Here he disclosed rare editorial acumen in a frank statement, analyzing minutely the qualities which the average American music-lover would seek in a journal, and promising that his program as di-rector of the enterprise would adequately satisfy those needs.

And so it becomes apparent that Deems Taylor the man is quite as important as Deems Taylor the composer. No record of his achievements in the latter capacity is complete without mention of the sterling qualities that he built within his own character. The chronicler of his history finds no evidence on this point more startling nor convincing than the happy, friendly relationship which exists between him and his publisher. Here indeed is a miracle, as witness the biographies of scores of the great composers of all times and observe the bickerings and transactions of distrust which have marked their dealings with the men who gave out their music to the world.

VI

Taylor has written more than fifty compositions, a full catalog of which is appended to this article. Without exception, each of these works, large or small, is of importance, and individual. Each bears analysis, but does not demand analysis for its enjoyment. While the individuality of his work is not essentially an idiom, and never a formula, there is always an atmosphere and a color that command attention. The music is thoughtful, yet spontaneous, reflective though objective; and so well constructed and designed that the structure does not impose itself on the listener.

Taylor's severest critics have accused him of lacking a true melodic gift. The most superficial study of his music should disprove this charge. The *Looking Glass* Suite and *The King's Henchman* abound in melodies interesting in themselves and ingeniously and logically developed. His best work has the quality of inevitability which is the supreme test of greatness in art, an inevitability which is never mere obviousness.

Comparisons are ever futile, and it is rarely profitable to compare one composer with another. Suffice it to say that we may claim Taylor as a native born composer, who needs no apology, no qualifying adjectives, no patriotic propaganda, no press agenting, and no circus methods for gaining recognition. He has gained recognition not because of or despite the fact that he is an American, but merely because he has written beautiful music, worthy to rank with the great works of the world.

On several occasions Taylor has given advice to young composers, either through interviews or articles written by himself.

The doctrine he expounds is tersely summarized in an article in "The Musical Digest," as follows:—

1. Get to be a professional.
2. Make everything you do count.
3. Try not to avoid criticism, and not to mind it.
4. Try not to make the same mistake twice.

This is not easily given advice to be disregarded by the giver; it is his own creed, reflected in every work in his list. He has written no "pot-boilers," made no concessions to the caprice of a fickle public, followed no easy paths to a facile popularity.

In an interview in "The Musical Observer" he once stated: "I think this country will produce some very bad composers and a few very great ones. Bad ones, because it is so easy to be popular here. You can please so many people by attaining a certain level—a level which requires very small gifts. A few great ones because anyone who has the nerve to be a good composer in this country and is so recognized, must be big enough to appeal to everybody, as the popular composer is bad enough to appeal to everybody."

VII

Taylor's songs and choral works are by-words on recital programs and his shorter works are household words in concert hall and studio. Those that have had the greatest vogue are *Mayday Carol* and *Captain Stratton's Fancy*.

Mayday Carol is a setting of an Essex folk-song in which the arranger has kept the warmth and simplicity of the original, and yet given it a sophisticated background. The harmonization is rich, and the counter melodies dextrously woven.

Captain Stratton's Fancy is a setting of the poem by John Masefield, and the combination has proved a song that has been the delight of hundreds of baritones. The spirit of the rum-loving pirate, "the old bold mate of Henry Morgan," is rollickingly emphasized by the music.

Banks o' Doon to a poem of Robert Burns, shows Taylor's lyric talent at its best. He has achieved the distinction of composing a melody which has all the attributes of a folk-song. There is simplicity, restraint, and yet a poignancy which brings out all the tender warmth of the exquisite poem.

For piano, Taylor has written only two pieces, *Two Studies in Rhythm*, Opus 5. These are a *Prelude* in 7-8 time, and a *Poem* in 5-8 time. The rhythms are never manufactured, or artificial; they are metric units written as conceived, spontaneous and natural. As in the 5-4 movement of the Tchaikovsky *Pathetique*, one forgets the unusual time divisions, because of the fluency of the rhythmic sequence.

As a writer of choral music, Taylor has earned an enviable distinction. Chief among his works for chorus are *The Chambered Nautilus*, a cantata for mixed chorus and orchestra, Opus 7; *The Highwayman*, a cantata for women's voices and orchestra, Opus 8; and the sixty arrangements for women's voices of *Traditional Airs*, which he made for the Schumann Club of New York. In reviewing these transcriptions, Sidney Grew, the English lecturer and critic, wrote as follows in "The Musical Standard" (London):

"In these arrangements of old-time pieces and folk-music Taylor seems to have his own idea of the psychology of the poems, and occasionally he is (to an Englishman's mind) drawn away from the poetical idea of a piece and controlled by the objective power of music. But this remark I make no more than tentatively, because to prove it would require a very thoroughgoing study of matters not within the range of a reviewer. He has a good contrapuntal sense, but is not at all interested in contrapuntal subtleties. His harmonic sense is free, yet he does little to disturb even the purist. In most of the numbers he achieves or retains atmosphere; and in disposing the texts among long notes in the accompanying parts he generally modifies the phrases so as to make verbal sense. On the other hand, he often brings in a group of voices with quite instrumental freedom, giving to these whatever words happen to be going at the moment in the leading part. One point will please singers, Taylor's arrangements have no meaningless reiteration of words, but are all intellectually clear and direct. Deems Taylor makes elaborate use of the humming voice, sometimes as choral accompaniment to a solo melody and sometimes as a meditative contrapuntal comment on the piece."

The experience he gained in writing for voices has stood him in good stead in his opera *The King's Henchman*, for his magnificent choruses are among its finest moments.

Of his orchestral works, the earliest was *The Siren Song*, Opus 2, written in 1912, but not performed until 1923, despite the fact that in 1913 it won the orchestral prize awarded by the National Federation of Women's Clubs. Taylor's opinion of the work is at variance with those of his fellow critics. At the time the Philharmonic played *The Siren Song*, as critic of the "World," he wrote as follows:

"We thought it a promising work with a certain freshness of feeling and a disarming simplicity of utterance that partly atoned for its lack of well-defined individuality. It followed the program with clarity and a degree of dramatic effectiveness, although the music did not seem to reach very far beneath the surface of the subtle and rather neurotic poem whose mood it aimed to express."

Henry T. Finck, writing in the "Post," valued the work more highly:

"Deems Taylor's *The Siren Song* is marked Opus 2. It would be a remarkably interesting composition if it were an Opus 20, or beyond. To be sure it betrays the influence of Wagner, but that's a most desirable influence. The three themes are distinctly recognizable and well worked out, with stunning climaxes and real dramatic and atmospheric sense for the sea and the siren. It is a fine mood picture and well worth keeping in the repertory."

The piece is written after a poem by Joseph Tiers, Jr., which tells of mariners hearing the siren's song, and either losing their souls, or resisting, being haunted by her voice forever. There are two principal themes, one representing the "Sea" and the other the "Siren," followed by a martial passage in lighter vein.

VIII

Through the Looking Glass was originally written in 1917-19 for strings, wind and piano, and performed by the New York Chamber Music Society. In 1921-22 Taylor rescored the suite for full orchestra, and it is now a regular feature of the repertoire of our leading orchestras. It is principally through this work that he first achieved his fame as a composer.

In reviewing the suite for the "New York Tribune," Law-rence Gilman wrote:

"He is wit enough to know that the peculiar distinction of Carroll's de-licious masterpiece is the mood of half tender, half mocking detachment in which it is conceived; and he preserves this balance in his music with extra-ordinary skill and felicity. He neither burlesques nor sentimentalizes his sub-ject. He touches it affectionately, even caressingly, as in the poetic and sensi-tive *Dedication;* but in his eye is a twinkle that is imperfectly suppressed. Incidentally, he has composed an admirable piece of music—distinguished in invention, ingenious in facture, and expertly scored."

The suite is, of course, based on Lewis Carroll's immortal nonsense tale *Through the Looking Glass,* and its four movements are selected from portions and episodes of the book.

The first movement is divided into two parts. It opens with the *Dedication,* and the score quotes the dedicatory verse of the author:

"Child of the pure, unclouded brow
And dreaming eyes of wonder!
Though time be fleet, and I and thou
Are half a life asunder,
Thy loving smile will surely hail
The love-gift of a fairy-tale."

A tenderly lyric theme, sung by a muted solo violin, is used to express the spirit of these lines:

This melody is next given to the clarinets, and then again to the strings as its brief development leads to the second part of the first movement, *The Garden of Live Flowers.* Here Alice finds herself surrounded by talkative flowers, who, to quote the tiger-lily, will speak "when there's anybody worth talking to." The music reflects the brisk chatter of the garden folk:

The second movement, *Jabberwocky*, is without doubt the masterpiece of the suite, for in it Taylor shows his skill as a tonal narrator, his humor, and his consummate mastery of orchestration. After a seven measure introduction, a solo clarinet establishes the "brillig" atmosphere with this motive:

The actual encounter with the Jabberwock is depicted by means of a fugue, started by the basses "burbling," which an English writer described as sounding like "Bach gone wrong."

The fight ends with a series of xylophone glissandos telling us how "through and through the vorpal blade went snicker-snack!" Then the dying agonies of the Jabberwock, a bassoon cadenza:

The hero comes "galumphing back" to this figure, played by the piano:

while the clarinet simultaneously sounds again the original heroic theme.

In the third movement, *Looking Glass Insects*, the composer again shows us his ability in orchestration, this time with more delicate touches. The several themes describe the bee-elephant, the rocking-horse-fly, the snap-dragon-fly, and the bread-and-butter-fly, but as the composer himself remarks, "there is no use trying to decide which insect any one of them stands for."

The fourth movement tells of *The White Knight*, the "toy Don Quixote, mild, chivalrous, ridiculous, and rather touching," who fell off in front when the horse stopped, and backwards when it went on again.

After a brief, galloping introduction, the first theme starts off bravely:

but falls out of the saddle before very long:

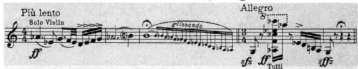

The first theme doubtless represents the Knight's own conception of himself as something of a dare-devil, but three hard falls necessitate his giving way to the somewhat sentimental and pathetic second theme, in which a solo violoncello paints him as he really was:

A page from the orchestra score
"Through the Looking Glass" - "Looking Glass Insects"

The two themes, in various forms, alternate until the close, when Alice waves her handkerchief as the Knight rides off, for he thought it would encourage him if she did.

American critics have been practically unanimous in their praise of the *Looking Glass* Suite, but when it was first played in London (1925) at the Queen's Hall Promenade Concerts, the English writers were by no means unqualified in their approval. A perusal of their comments almost gives one the impression that they resented an American's attempt to depict such characteristically British humor.

The reviewer of the "Evening Standard" said: ". . . his suite is curiously uneven. In places it is heavy and long-winded; Lewis Carroll was neither."

The critic of the "Daily Express" was more complimentary, as was the "Daily Sketch," but the writer for the "Morning Post" stated:

". . . his capacity for detail misleads him. Instead of creating a vision by a wave of his hand, he fills in his picture inch by inch, carefully balancing his outlines and masses, and filling the whole of his rectangle with subject matter. A good musician, no doubt, but far from catching the white rabbit."

With these adverse comments we cannot agree. The pages of the Suite are not smothered with detail, the episodes and pictures of the book are impressions clearly delineated, and painted with a sparkle and brilliance that prove irresistible and dazzling.

The *Portrait of a Lady* was composed shortly after the *Looking Glass* Suite, and rewritten in 1924. Ernest Newman wrote of it in the "Post":

". . . he stood up like a man to Schubert, Juon and Novak; and at the end of the concert only he and Schubert had survived."

Lawrence Gilman of the "Tribune" said:

"Out of the empty, agitated air he conjured an image that had line and color and background, substance and character; something coherent, vivid, personal. And when he was through . . . we found ourselves richer by an experience and a possession, and wondering, as we never fail to do, at the mysterious potency of the art of music."

The work was composed for strings, wood-wind and piano, and, according to the composer, fol ows no definite program, but was designed to be "somewhat analogous to what a painter would call an ideal head; an attempt to convey the impression of a human personality in terms of music." According to the music this personality has two phases: one grave, meditative and tender, the other capricious and somewhat worldly. The music has warmth and depth, and as W. J. Henderson wrote in the "Sun," "makes one wish to see the woman."

The incidental music to *Beggar on Horseback* included the delightful pantomime *A Kiss in Xanadu*, to a scenario by Winthrop Ames. Taylor wrote this for two pianos, and we may well hope that he carries out his intention of scoring it for orchestra.

The music radiates moonlight and romance, and its humor enhances the spirit of satire. The opening measures establish the atmosphere with a 5-4 theme:

The Royal Bedchamber episode is ushered in with this vigorous motive:

The Princess is introduced with a Valse:

In the public park incident, a stirring little march:

leads to a more coquettish mood:

The third scene finishes as the pantomime began, with a colorful reminiscence of the opening themes.

Taylor's next important work is *Jurgen*, a symphonic work for full orchestra, based on Cabell's famous novel. His own statement of his aims in regard to it are as follows:

"*Jurgen* was originally planned as an orchestral suite that would follow as faithfully as possible the sequence of events in James Branch Cabell's book. But when I started work on the music it became increasingly obvious that such a program was not only impracticable, but hardly to the point. It would take a cycle of suites to do adequate justice to the bewildering multitude of scenes, characters and episodes with which the pages of *Jurgen* are crowded. Moreover, the importance of Cabell's romance as a work of art lies, not in its qualities as a diverting tale of amorous adventure, but in the vividness, the sardonic gusto, the humor and wisdom and pathetic beauty with which the tale is told.

"So, *Jurgen*, annotated in terms of music, has come to be concerned much more with the man Jurgen than with his deeds. In brief, I have tried to show Jurgen, facing the unanswerable riddle of why things are as they are; Jurgen 'clad in the armor of his hurt', spinning giddily through life, strutting, posturing, fighting, loving, pretending; Jurgen proclaiming himself count, duke, king, emperor, god; Jurgen, beaten at last by the pathos and mystery of life, bidding farewell to that dream of beauty, which he had the vision to see, but not the strength to follow."

Continuing his explanation of the work, Taylor writes:

"The music is built upon four themes. The first of these, which is Jurgen's own, is announced at the outset, in its broadest and vaguest form, by the bass

clarinet. The second follows immediately, a simple series of major and minor triads given out in turn by muted strings and muted brass. Its first appearance

is also the first appearance of the third theme, which is really only a motto of four notes in length, which rises a major second and falls back a minor second.

Neither of these themes can be assigned a very specific significance. Theme number two might be taken as symbolic of Koshchei, the Deathless, who made things as they are, just as theme number three is a reminder of Mother Sereda, who bleaches the color out of all things and renders life generally futile. The fourth theme, broadly lyric, is first heard in the cellos, at the beginning of the love scene that follows the first development of Jurgen's theme. This might

be called—again not too literally—Dorothy la Désirée, or Helen of Troy, or the vision of beauty; or what you will."

Jurgen's performance in 1925 by the Symphony Society was met with mixed emotions on the part of the press reviewers. Mr. Chotzinoff, Taylor's successor on the "World," was laudatory with reservations; Mr. Henderson of the "Sun" felt that the score was too long, but added that this may have been because it followed Kallinikoff and Brahms on a lengthy program. He wrote:

"It is a broadly painted musical canvas which loses itself just a little too much in the philosophical depths of Jurgen's nature. The reflective pages in the score are a little longer than the reflective mood of a typical audience. These pages are saturated with feeling, with poetic character, with musical emotion; but they are pages to be read in the shadows of the twilight. . . . These pages Mr. Taylor has composed with a splendid verve, with brilliant thematic conception, with opulence of color and his own unquenchable spirit of defiant humor. There is music in every page, music that should bring gladness to the American music lover in that it was made by an American."

IX

No better introduction to a discussion of *The King's Henchman* could be found than another quotation from Mr. Gilman, written in the "Tribune" on the occasion of the opera's première at the Metropolitan:

"Thus we came to the end of the best American opera we have ever heard, and so easily the best of the ten produced by Mr. Gatti-Casazza at the Metropolitan that there is none other in the running. (Mr. Taylor has woven a deft and often lovely sounding score about a superb poetic text)—a text pithy and glamorous and full of character; rich in humor and dramatic force, rich in imagery that is often startling in its beauty and its swift felicity. And this text is apt for voices or for viols. It clamors for vocal utterance and for enforcement by the instruments of the mirroring orchestra.

(Mr. Taylor's score is in the worthiest sense theatrically planned and developed.) It is obvious that he wrote with his eye on the stage, with his intelligence responsive to its tyrannous requirements. Furthermore, he has given musical voice to English words which, sung from the stage, are not only heard, but are expressive, and fitting, and often beautiful. The music, as music, "sounds"; (it fills the ear, is richly textured, mellifluous, has grace and movement and flexibility. It is the writing of an expert craftsman, an artist of sensibility and warm responsiveness.)'

For her libretto, Miss Millay went to the England of the ninth century for her setting, and, in authentic Anglo-Saxon verbiage tells us the story of Eadgar, King of England, a widower who wishes a second wife. Like King Mark in *Tristan*, he dispatches a trusted retainer, Aethelwold, to bring to him Aelfrida, daughter of the Thane of Devon, of whose beauty he has heard. Like Tristan and like John Alden, Aethelwold falls in love with the lady himself, and tragedy is inevitable.

It has often been remarked that the weaker the libretto, the better the opera. If any proof were needed to challenge so obvious a fallacy, *The King's Henchman* provides it, for here is a poetic drama which of itself stands in perfect security. In the "Tribune" Elinor Wylie wrote, after reading the poem:

"If this is not lyric dialogue of the true poetic water, why then has it such a magic in it that it has turned me into a fool and my taste into untruth."

The story is grippingly told, the tragedy of it appalling, and the characters are limned with an insight that makes them real people, actuated by motives beyond their control.

Because of his wisdom in choosing his librettist, Taylor commenced his work with a drama that cried out for musical setting, for a tonal accompaniment to its atmosphere, and to the thoughts and actions of its people; and if in the making of it he has fallen under the spell of Wagner's musical delineation of the kindred love-drama *Tristan*, or of Debussy, whose love scene in *Pelleas* is akin to the forest scene in *The King's Henchman*, who can blame him, for who could have avoided it? Taylor himself has said:

"Its form has undoubtedly been influenced by the methods of past masters . . . ; as to that, I can only hope that its spiritual grandfather may turn out to be Wagner rather than Puccini."

The score of *The King's Henchman* makes frequent use of the *leit-motif*, to represent both actual characters, and abstract conceptions. The short prelude opens with the King (Eadgar) motive:

Con brio

This is frequently found, later in the action, in a broader, more lyric form:

After a brief development, the curtain rises and reveals the hall of King Eadgar's castle with the King and his nobles seated at the table, while Maccus, the harper, sings of deeds of valor. Then follows a choral response, with the words:

> "Be the day far off, O harper
> When thy harp is unstrung!
> And thy hand still,
> And thy song sung."

The Aelfrida motive is first introduced while she is being discussed as the King's prospective bride:

When Aethelwold is mentioned as the one to get her, we hear his sturdy motive:

which is continued and developed while the knights dwell on his fitness for the task, for was it not true that

> "He shunneth a fair maid
> As she were a foul marten
> And should a wench but breathe
> upon him in the dark,
> He would bury himself till the
> smell of her were off him!"

While they are talking about Aethelwold he enters, and the expedition is planned, the henchman receives his final instructions, the Archbishop gives his reluctant blessing, and, as the pledge is sealed we first hear the pledge motive:

which is quoted frequently throughout the opera. As the knights drink Aethelwold's health and bid him godspeed, there comes a rousing choral arrangement of the only folk-song used in the entire work:

and so on, through others of the Caesars involved in the Roman invasion of England: Claudius and Hadrian. The handling of voices and orchestra in this chorus is the most stunning choral writing Taylor has ever achieved. After this song, Aethelwold's horse is brought in and he takes his departure as the curtain falls, and the orchestra sounds the Aethelwold motive as a salvo.

X

The second act is chiefly an extended love scene, and the impassioned prelude, commencing with the Aethelwold motive, establishes the mood and atmosphere. As the curtain rises, a forest in Devon is discovered, on the Eve of All Hallow Mass. A thick fog causes Aethelwold and Maccus, who accompanies him, to lose their way and become separated. The orchestra, with muted strings, weaves a background of forest murmurings as Aethelwold stretches himself beneath an oak. As he falls asleep a light appears, and we hear a theme which is later associated with the love scene:

As Aelfrida enters with a lantern we again hear her motive. She had come to practice a magic spell, hoping that her incantation would bring her a lover. As she hums the tune, "white-thorn, black-thorn, holy-bough, speed-well," a ghostly chorus behind the scenes answers her. As the mist clears, the moonlight falls upon Aethelwold, and she kisses him. As he arises they fall in each other's arms; and then begins one of the most beautiful love duets in the literature of music. It is based on the principal love-theme of the opera:

They tell each other their names, and Aethelwold horror-stricken learns who she is. As Aelfrida leaves him, to return in a moment, the henchman is left alone to make his decision. The orchestra tells us of his inner strife, we hear reminders of the King's motive, and the pledge; he tries to flee, but her voice detains him, and as Maccus appears seeking him, he gives way to his temptation and dispatches his harper to the King, with this message:

"Maccus, go back unto the King,
And say to him:
That I have seen the maiden,
And found her nothing fair.
A come y maid enough, and friendly spoken,
But nothing for the King.
Further say:
That whereas the Thane of Devon,
 the lady's father,
Is rich in lands and kine;
And whereas the Lord Aethelwold
Spare the King's love, hath little
 else beside,—
The blessing of King Eadgar is
 besought
Upon the wedding of Lord Aethelwold
Unto the maid Aelfrida."

As Maccus departs, Aethelwold turns to Aelfrida, saying:
"Now shall I look no more beyond thine eyes."

Both words and music, throughout the act, portray Aethel-wold's intense desire to be loyal to his King, but show the complete inability of almost any man to resist the spell woven by the forest. The music achieves a compelling mood of rapturous lyricism, and its broadly drawn phrases of sensuous melody build up magnificently to the climax of the act.

XI

The prelude to the third act starts with a tune, in the folk-song manner, sung by the wood-winds:

As the curtain rises we find Ase, Aelfrida's serving maid, singing while she spins in the hall of Ordgar's house, where Aethelwold is living with his bride. Then comes a tense scene between Aelfrida and Aethelwold, for she is fretted by her preoccupation with the cares of the household, and not wholly content with a husband whose unconfessed treachery must have caused him many sleepless nights. Aethelwold accordingly plans that they shall leave Devon immediately, and go to Ghent in Flanders where Aelfrida would henceforth go "in sighing silk and gossamer and hooded in beaver-fell." As they sing farewell to Devon the orchestra commences a theme which is heard at different times throughout the act, a melody of great beauty and pathos:

But it is too late, for the King is at that moment at the gates, come on a friendly visit. Aethelwold confesses his deception to his wife:

> "Yea, my child, 'tis true enough.
> I lied to Eadgar,
> Saying thou were little fair.
> Oh, the good smack of truth on
>   the tongue again,
> After a winter of lies."

He then bids Aelfrida help him keep up his deception to the King, and to retire and dim her beauty:

> "Go now, and darken thy cheek
> with the sap of the walnut,
> And dust thy hair with the meal
> of the wheat,—
> Be foul, be bent, be weathered,
> And keep thy bower, that none may
> see thee,
> But myself and the King!"

Aelfrida departs to do his bidding—or so Aethelwold thinks.

Eadgar and his men enter singing the folk-song of the first act. As he greets Aethelwold, and asks to be taken to the bride, Aelfrida suddenly appears in the doorway, in all her jewels, proud, beautiful and splendid. Eadgar's arm slowly drops from Aethelwold's shoulders, and the orchestra in a discordant crash sounds the pledge motive.

After Eadgar's sorrowful rebuke, Aethelwold plunges his dagger into his breast, and a brief threnody is spoken by the King. Then follows the choral ending of the opera, with the King intoning his lament against the chorus of retainers and woodsmen, and the orchestra playing a passage, reminiscent of the "farewell to Devon" theme!—

As the retainers lift the body of Aethelwold and bear it away, the orchestra again plays the pledge motive, and the curtain falls.

Facsimile page from the manuscript orchestra score
"The King's Henchman"—Act III

LIST OF COMPOSITIONS BY DEEMS TAYLOR

NOTE:—The numbers before each group of titles refer to the publisher.

LYRIC DRAMA

(1) **The King's Henchman** (*Edna St. Vincent Millay*), **Op. 19**
In three acts

CHAMBER MUSIC AND ORCHESTRA

(1) **The Siren Song, Op. 2**
Symphonic Poem for Orchestra
(1) **Through the Looking-Glass, Op. 12** (*Five Pictures from Lewis Carroll*)
1a Dedication
1b The Garden of Live Flowers
2. Jabberwocky
3. Looking Glass Insects
4. The White Knight
Suite for
Symphony orchestra
Symphony orchestra—reduced
Strings, wind and piano
(1) **The Portrait of a Lady, Op. 14**
Rhapsody for strings, wind and piano
(1) **Jurgen, Op. 17**
Symphonic poem for orchestra
(1) **Circus Day, Op. 18**
Suite for jazz orchestra (*Scored by Ferdie Grofé*)
For symphony orchestra (*Scored by the composer*)

CHORAL-CANTATAS

(2) **The Chambered Nautilus** (*Oliver Wendell Holmes*), **Op. 7**
For mixed voices and orchestra
(2) **The Highwayman** (*Alfred Noyes*), **Op. 8**
For women's voices and orchestra
Also for mixed voices and orchestra

PART-SONGS

(2) **May Eve** (*Thomas S. Jones*), **Op. 11, No. 1,** S.S.A.A.
(1) **Tricolor** (*Paul Scott Mowrer*), **Op. 11, No. 2,** S.S.A.A. T.T.B.B.
(1) **Valse Ariette** (*Humming chorus*), **Op. 11, No. 3,** S.S.A.A.
(1) **Banks o'Doon** (*Robert Burns*), S.S.A. (arranged)
(1) **Plantation Love Song** ("My Rose") (*Ruth McEnery Stuart*), S.S.A.A. T.T.B.B. (arranged)
(5) **Little Dancing Leaves** (*Lucy Larcom*), Unison
(5) **The Day Is Done** (*H. W. Longfellow*), S.S.A.
(5) **Old Ironsides** (*Oliver Wendell Holmes*), S.S.A.B.
(Written for the Universal School Music Series)

(1) J. FISCHER & BRO., New York.   (2) OLIVER DITSON CO., Boston, Mass.   (5) HINDS, HAYDEN & ELDREDGE, INC., New York.

LIST OF COMPOSITIONS BY DEEMS TAYLOR

HARMONIZATIONS AND TRANSCRIPTIONS

(1) **Armenian Folksongs:**
By the Cradle, S.S.A.
Heart-Longings, S.S.A.
My Grief, S.S.A.
The Well-Beloved, S.S.A. T.T.B.B. S.A.T.B.

(1) **Belgian Folksongs:**
The Faithless Lover (L'Abandonnée), S.S.A.
Grizzly, Grumpy Granny (La Boiteuse), S.S.A.
In the Country (La Vie Rustique), S.S.A.
The Siesta (La Sieste), S.S.A.

(1) **Breton Folksongs:**
Before the Shrine (Disons le Chapelet), S.S.A.A. T.T.B.B. S.A.T.B.
The Sabot-Maker (Le Sabotier), S.S.A.
The Soul's Departure (Le Départ de l'Ame), S.S.A.
The Wedding Dress (La Petite Robe), S.S.A.

(1) **Czecho-Slovak Folksongs:**
Good Night (Dobru Noc), S.S.A.
Lightning Now Flashes (Nad Tatrou sa Blyska), S.S.A.
Song to Bohemia (Tesme se Blahou Nadeji), S.S.A.
Wake Thee, Now, Dearest (Pridi ty Suhajko), S.S.A.
Waters Ripple and Flow (Tece Voda, Tece), S.S.A. T.T.B.B.
S.A.T.B.

(1) **English Folksongs:**
The Loyal Lover, S.S.A.A. S.A.T.B.
Mayday Carol, S.A. S.S.A. S.S.A.A. S.A.B. T.T.B.B. S.A.T.B.
My Johnny Was a Shoemaker, S.S.A. T.T.B.B. S.A.T.B.
Twenty, Eighteen, S.S.A. T.T.B.B. S.A.T.B.

(1) **Scotch Songs:**
Ae Fond Kiss, S.S.A.A.
Hame, Hame, Hame, S.S.A.A. T.T.B.B.
Rantin', Rovin' Robin, S.S.A.A.
Whistle, My Lad, S.S.A.A.

ARRANGEMENTS

(2) —————	Southern Medley, S.S.A.A.
(1) J. S. Bach	Air (Humming Chorus), Unison
(1) G. B. Bassani	Rest and Slumber (Posate, Dormite), S.S.A.A.
(1) G. M. Bononcini	Turn Not From Me (Non V'Ascondete), S.S.A.
(3) H. T. Burleigh	De Gospel Train, S.S.A.
	Hard Trials, S.S.A.
	Heav'n, Heav'n, S.S.A.

(1) J. FISCHER & BRO., New York.   (2) OLIVER DITSON CO., Boston, Mass.   (3) G. RICORDI & CO., New York.

LIST OF COMPOSITIONS BY DEEMS TAYLOR

(1) **J. Brahms**	**Crimson Clouds** (Rothe Abendwolken), S.S.A.A.
	Gypsy Minstrel (He, Zigeuner), S.S.A.A.
	The Mountains Are Cold (Die Berge sind Spitz), S.S.A.A.
	Now Sounds the Harp (Es Tönt ein Harfenklang), S.S.A.
	When Sweetly Blossom Roses (Nun steh'n die Rosen), S.S.A.
(1) **G. Caccini**	**Amaryllis My Fair One** (Amarilli, Mia Bella), S.S.A.A.
(1) **M. A. Cesti**	**Where Sleeps My Beloved** (Intorno all' Idol Mio), S.S.A.A.
(1) **E. Chausson**	**The Humming Bird** (Le Colibri), S.S.A.A.
(1) **C. Debussy**	**Afterglow** (Beau Soir), S.S.A.
(1) **J. Des Pres**	**What Sorrow Mine** (J'ay Mil Regrets), S.S.A.A.
(3) **S. Donaudy**	**Fragrant Groves and Flowery Meadows** (Freschi Luoghi, Prati Aulenti), S.S.A.
	Oh, Hasten, Beloved (Madonna Renzuola), S S.A.A.
	O, Likeness, Dim and Faded (Vaghissima Sembianza), S.S.A.
	O, Vanished Loveliness (O Del Mio Amato Ben), S.S.A.
	Spring Song (Sorge il Sol!), S.S.A.
	The Lover's Tale (Ognun Ripicchia e Nicchia), S.S.A.
	'Tis Love That Sets Me Singing (Amor Mi Fa Cantare), S.S.A.
	When You Love's Game Were Learning (Quand' il tuo Diavol Nacque), S S.A.
(1) **H F. Duparc**	**A Sigh** (Soupir), S.S.A.A.
(1) **F. Durante**	**Dance, Little Maid** (Danza, Danza), S.S.A.
	Virgin, All of Love (Vergin, Tutto Amor), S.S.A.
(1) **G. B. Fasolo**	**Give Me Peace** (Cangia, Cangia), S.S.A.
(1) **G. Fauré**	**After a Dream** (Après un Reve), S.S.A.A.
	The Cradles (Les Berceaux), S.S.A.A.
(1) **John of Fornsete**	**Sumer Is Icumen In**, S.S.S.S.A.A.
(2) **C. Forsyth**	**From the Hills of Dream**, S.S.A.A.
French:	
(1) **XII. Century**	**La Bele Yolans** (Fair Yolanthe), S.S.A.
	La Reine d'Avril (The Queen of April), S.S.A.A.

(1) J. Fischer & Bro., New York. (2) Oliver Ditson Co., Boston, Mass. (3) G. Ricordi & Co., New York.

LIST OF COMPOSITIONS BY DEEMS TAYLOR

(1) XIV. Century	**Je Suis Trop Jeunette** (Nay, My Years Are Tender), S.S.A.A.
(1) XVII. Century	**Le Berger Discret** (The Timid Shepherd), S.S.A.A.
(1) XVIII. Century	**Ah, Mon Berger** (Shepherd Mine Own), S.S.A.A.
	Chaque Chose à Son Temps (Everything Has Its Time), S.S.A.A.
	La Chanson du Tambourineur (The Drummer-Boy's Song), S.S.A.A.
	Les Belles Manières (The Ways of the World), S.S.A.A.
(1) **J. Gallus**	**O Salutaris**, S.S.A.A.
(1) **German Folksong**	**Spinnerliedchen** (Spinning Song), S.S.A.A.
(2) **R. M. Gliere**	**Ah, Twine No Blossoms**, S.S.A.A.
(1) **E. Grieg**	**Are They Tears, Beloved?** (Warum schimmert dein Auge?), S.S.A.
	Christmas Snow (Neige de Noel), S.S.A.A.
	A Dream (Ein Traum), S.S.A.A.
	Rosebud (Rosenknospe), S.S.A.
(1) **J. L. Hatton**	**To Anthea**, S.S.A.
(1) **Dorothy Herbert**	**After Sunset**, S.S.A.
	The Song of Desire, S.S.A.
(1) **Hungarian Folksongs**	**For But One** (Nur eine schönes Mädchen), S.S.A.
	O Marie (Marishka), S.S.A.
	Whither Going Shepherd? (Sag' Mir Csikos), S.S.A.
	Play, O Gypsy (Spiell Zigeuner), S.S.A.
(1) **Eastwood Lane**	**The Little Fisherman**, S.S.A.A.
Latin:	
(1) XIV. Century	**Concordi Laetitia** (Hymn to the Virgin), S.S.A.A. T.T.B.B. S.A.T.B.
(1) **J. B. de Lully**	**Lonely Wood** (Bois Epais), S.S.A.
(4) **Ethelbert Nevin**	**The Land of Heart's Desire** Cantata, Baritone Solo, S.S.A.
(1) **G. P. da Palestrina**	**Sub Tuum**, S.S.A.
	O Bone Jesu, S.S.A.A.
(2) **Edna R. Park**	**The Romaika**, S.S.A.
(3) **G. Puccini**	**Love and Music** (Vissi d'Arte), S.S.A.
	One Fine Day (Un Bel Di), S.S.A.
(1) **S. Rachmaninoff**	**Cry of Russia** (A Lament), Vocalise, S.S.A.A.
(2) **N. Rimsky-Korsakoff**	**Nightingale and the Rose**, S.S.A.

(1) J. FISCHER & BRO., New York. (2) OLIVER DITSON Co., Boston, Mass. (3) G. RICORDI & Co., New York. (4) THE JOHN CHURCH Co., Cincinnati, Ohio.

(3) **Geni Sadero**	**Beautiful Vine** (Pampina Pampinedda), S.S.A.
	Hush-A-By (Era la Vo), S.S.A.
	My Love, My Darling (Curi, Curuzzu), S.S.A.
	Out Seaward (In Mezo al Mar), S.S.A.
	Rock-a-Bye Baby Mine (Fa la Nana Bambin), S.S.A.
(1) **A. Scarlatti**	**If Florindo Be Faithful** (Se Florindo e Fedele), S.S.A.
(1) **R. Schumann**	**Bride's Song** (Lied der Braut), S.S.A.A.
	Dedication (Widmung), S.S.A.A.
(1) **C. Sinding**	**Anemone,** S.S.A.A.
(1) **Percy Rector Stephens**	**To the Spirit of Music,** S.S.A.A. T.T.B.B. S.A.T.B.
(1) **R. Strauss**	**Devotion** (Zueignung), S.S.A.
(1) **T. L. da Vittoria**	**Ave Maria,** S.S.A.A.
(1) **Hugo Wolf**	**Insatiable Love** (Nimmersatte Liebe), S.S.A.
	The Drummer-Boy (Der Tambour), S.S.A.

SONGS

(2) **Witch Woman** (*Celia Harris*), **Op. 3**

(1) **Plantation Love Song** ("My Rose"), (*Ruth McEnery Stuart*) **Op. 6**

(2) **The City of Joy** (*Charles Hanson Towne*), **Op. 9.** A Song Cycle

    1. Spring in Town

    2. Poor . . .

    3. . . . But Happy

    4. The Roof Garden

    5. Home!

(2) **Time Enough** (*Brian Hooker*), **Op. 10, No. 1**

(1) **The Rivals** (*James Stephens*), **Op. 13, No. 1**

    A Song for Lovers (*James Stephens*), **Op. 13, No. 2**

    The Messenger (*James Stephens*), **Op. 13, No. 3**

(1) **Traditional Airs.** (Harmonized by Deems Taylor) **Op. 15**

    1. La Bele Yolans (Fair Yolanthe)

    2. Je Suis Trop Jeunette (Nay, My Years Are Tender)

    3. La Sieste (The Siesta)

    4. L'Abandonnée (The Faithless Lover)

    5. La Vie Rustique (In the Country)

    6. Rantin', Rovin' Robin

    7. Ae Fond Kiss

    8. Hame, Hame, Hame

    9. Mayday Carol

    10. Twenty, Eighteen

    11. The Loyal Lover

(1) J. FISCHER & BRO., New York.   (2) OLIVER DITSON Co., Boston, Mass.   (3) G. RICORDI & CO., New York.

12. Le Départ de l'Ame (The Soul's Departure)
13. Les Belles Manières (The Ways of the World)
14. La Petite Robe (The Wedding Dress)
(1) **Captain Stratton's Fancy** (*John Masefield*)
(1) **The Banks o'Doon** (*Robert Burns*)

PIANO

(1) **A Kiss in Xanadu.** Pantomine Music. **Op. 16**
(1) **Two Studies in Rhythm. Op. 5**
    1. Prelude 2. Poem

ORGAN

(1) **Dedication.** From "Through the Looking Glass." Transcribed by Charles M. Courboin

---

INCIDENTAL MUSIC

"Liliom." Produced in New York by Theatre Guild

"Will Shakespeare." Produced in New York by Winthrop Ames

"Humoresque." Produced in New York by George Tyler

"Rita Coventry." Produced in New York by Brock Pemberton

"The Adding Machine." Produced in New York by Theatre Guild

"Casanova." Produced in New York by Gilbert Miller

"Beggar on Horseback." Produced in New York by Winthrop Ames
(Incidental music includes the pantomime "A Kiss in Xanadu.")

---

(1) J. FISCHER & BRO., New York.

This Series of Brochures will include the following American Composers

ALEXANDER RUSSELL*
EASTWOOD LANE*
JAMES P. DUNN*
A. WALTER KRAMER*
DEEMS TAYLOR*

In Preparation:

MORTIMER WILSON
WALTER GOLDE
CHARLES WAKEFIELD CADMAN
HOWARD D. McKINNEY
CARL McKINLEY
SAMUEL RICHARDS GAINES
FRANZ C. BORNSCHEIN
J. W. CLOKEY
FAY FOSTER
LILY STRICKLAND
HELEN DALLAM

and others

---

*Now available

Date Due

Library Bureau Cat. No. 1137

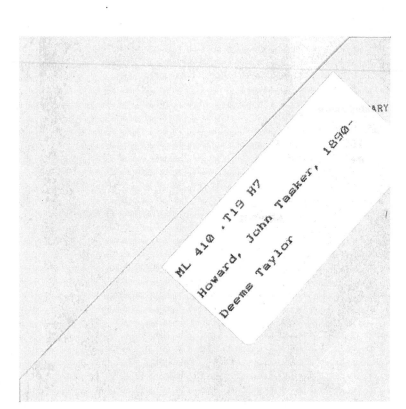

CPSIA information can be obtained
at www.ICGtesting.com
Printed in the USA
BVHW050944060223
657963BV00009B/667

9 781015 243019